D1596353

HAPPY
ANNIVERSARY

The C. R. Gibson Company
Norwalk, Connecticut

IT ALL ADDS UP

So many miles of coffee,
So many smiles and tears,
So many shining moments
As days blend into years.

So many morning kisses,
So many nighttime hugs,
So many walks and so many talks
Shared by those who love.

Joys cannot be counted,
And lovers don't keep score.
With every day that passes
Love is growing more and more.

Barbara Shook Hazen

SONG FOR A MARRIAGE

Now from all mountains you come down
Radiant after those reaches of despair
Which you climbed once on courage alone,
A footstep's span from the dreadful air.
Now from interminable empty seas
Where the unwavering compass was your hope,
You land at last as radiant as those
Saints who discover a mysterious home,
Where out of conflict the most difficult joys
Like poetry, like love, search and find poise.
You give us a new world. Tenderness flows
Out from your hands like some amazing news.
And in this marriage rooted deep in trust
We bless a legend we had almost lost,
The miracle of balance and of gentleness
That steadfast love may slowly bring to pass.

May Sarton

THE GREATEST OF ALL ADVENTURES

Mrs. Norman Vincent Peale answers a college senior who questions marriage.

Here's how it all began . . .

The young woman who stood up at the back of the room was a college senior—dark-haired, handsome, sophisticated, a little scornful. "Mrs. Peale," she said, "a moment ago when someone asked you what you considered the greatest career for a woman, you said marriage—right? Well, let's be honest, shall we? It's my opinion—and the opinion, I'd say, of most of my friends—that marriage as an institution is obsolete." She shook back her dark hair in a defiant gesture. "We're not blind, Mrs. Peale. We look around and we see what marriage does to people and we don't like what we see. I think when I say these things I'm speaking for a large part of my generation. Do you have any answer?"

All the bright young faces swung in my direction, and I took a deep breath. It was true. I had said that in my opinion marriage was the greatest career a woman could have. I had agreed that a woman might have other stimulating and important jobs, but none was so difficult and demanding, so exciting and potentially rewarding as the job of living with a man, studying him, supporting him, liberating his strengths, compensating for his weaknesses, making his whole mechanism soar and sing the way it was designed to do. I had said this because I believed it completely, but I hadn't expected a challenge quite so blunt and harsh as this one. Modern marriage, this handsome young woman was saying, was a fraud and a mockery—and she wanted to know if I had an answer.

"Yes," I said to her quietly, "I have an answer, because I'm

in the process of living it. I consider myself one of the most fortunate women alive. Why? Because I am totally married to a man in every sense of the word: physically, emotionally, intellectually, spiritually. We're so close that you couldn't put a knife blade between us. I need him and depend on him completely. He completely needs and depends on me. We're not two lonely, competing individuals. We're one integrated, mutually responsive, mutually supportive organism—and this is such a marvelous and joyous thing that nothing else in life can even approach it. It's the greatest of all adventures, but *you'll* never know it. You'll never even come within shouting distance of it if you maintain the attitudes and the code of conduct you've adopted."

"I don't see why not," she said, but her voice had lost some of its conviction. "Why can't a man-woman relationship be just as meaningful outside of marriage as in it?"

"Because," I told her, "it doesn't have the key ingredients. It doesn't have the commitment. It doesn't have the permanence. It can never achieve the depth that comes from total sharing, from working together toward common goals year after year, from knowing that you're playing the game for keeps. Do you think my husband and I have achieved the relationship we have just by thinking happy thoughts or waving a wand? Don't be absurd! We fought for this relationship! We hammered it out on the anvil of joy and sorrow, of pain and problems—yes, at times, of discouragement and disagreement. But we never thought of marriage as a trap. We thought of it as a privilege. And there's quite a difference!"

WHY DO PEOPLE MARRY?

For love, for affection, for friendship. Men's and women's emotional needs are complementary. Both sexes need the love, affection, and friendship of the other.
No one ever suffered from a surfeit of love. And true love in a liberated marriage is not smother love.
No one was ever exploited by honest affection.
No one should be expected to go through life without a best friend. A husband (and a wife) can be the best friend of all.

Dr. Joyce Brothers

DREAM'S END

So fair, so beautiful, so young,
Yours was the song my heart had sung;
Yours the lips my lips had kissed,
Before I knew you did exist;

The hands I yearned for as a child,
The smile I sought to soothe the wild
Restless stirrings in my breast;
The haven where I longed to rest.

You were the dream I dreamed alone.
Now you are here: my hearth, my home.

Barbara Shook Hazen

A NIGHT TO REMEMBER

Minor misunderstandings make memories. Lawrence Welk recalls one on a combined anniversary/business trip to Hawaii.

Fern likes Hawaii—but there were a few hours there when I was convinced she didn't like it at all, or else she didn't like me! At the time we made the trip, we were celebrating our forty-second wedding anniversary, so it seemed like a good chance for a second honeymoon. And as we flew in over the Islands they looked as lovely as we remembered. Fern was a little fatigued when we arrived, so after dinner that night she excused herself and went up to bed. I stayed on for the business on hand. It was after midnight when I said goodnight and went up to our suite. The door was locked, and I couldn't get it open no matter how hard I tried. Fern had evidently put the inside lock on, and no amount of fiddling around with my key could get it open. I rattled and knocked and hissed "Fern, Fern!" as loudly as I dared. Nothing worked. Finally I went downstairs and called her on the house phone. It rang and rang, but no answer. In desperation I went to the desk clerk and told him my troubles and he roused out the manager who took me back upstairs and opened the door with his master key. I tiptoed across the vast living room and into our bedroom, where just as I expected, Fern was sound asleep.

Next morning, in honor of the occasion, I ordered breakfast in our room. The waiter served it at a table in front of the floor-to-ceiling windows overlooking the sparkling sea below, with Diamond Head in the distance, outlined sharply against the clear, blue sky. As we ate, the soft ocean breeze billowed the glass curtains and carried in the scent of pikaki and Hawaiian ginger flowers, and if I'd staged the whole

thing myself I could never have come up with a prettier setting. So, after breakfast, I cleared my throat and made a little speech. "Fern," I said, "as you know, this is our wedding anniversary."

She nodded.

"Well," I said, "I just want to tell you what you've meant to me all these years. You've been a . . . a wonderful wife, in every way."

She smiled, pleased.

"You've given me three fine children," I went on. "And you've always made our home such a pleasant, happy place to be." She smiled again, turning a little pink. "Fern," I added, really getting warmed up to the subject, "you've always kept everything so neat, so clean! In fact, you're the cleanest person I know!"

She was really smiling now, just beaming. "Why . . . thank you, Lawrence."

"And, Fern, you've always been so . . . well, so considerate, and loving with me."

She smiled even wider, really enjoying this whole tribute. "That's very nice."

"Fern?"

"Yes, Lawrence?"

"Why did you lock me out of our room last night?"

There was a second act to this little comedy. After we'd talked about it and had a good laugh, I said, "Fern, one thing puzzles me. When I called you from the lobby the phone rang and rang. Were you that sound asleep, you didn't hear it?"

"Oh, sure," she said matter-of-factly. "I heard it. But I just figured it would be for you anyway—so I'd let you answer it!"

GOING CONCERN

Suppose my wife and I are sitting.
I'm reading, maybe, and she's knitting.
I'm nicely settled, hate to stir;
The same, no doubt, is true of her.
Comes now a ring upon the phone,
Or Spots wants out, to dig a bone,
Or Junior calls, demands a drink,
Or water's dripping in the sink.
A thoughtful soul, I drop my book
And give my wife a tender look.
"I'll go, my dear. Sit still," I say,
But not until she's on her way.

Richard Armour

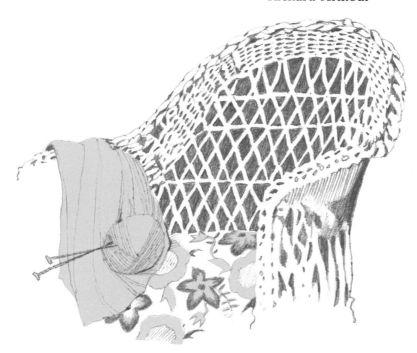

MY OWN RULES FOR A HAPPY MARRIAGE

Nobody, I hasten to announce, has asked me to formulate a set of rules for the perpetuation of marital bliss. The idea just came to me one day; brooding on the general subject of Husbands and Wives, I found myself compiling my own Rules for a Happy Marriage.

Rule One: Neither party to a sacred union should run down, disparage, or badmouth the other's former girls or beaux, as the case may be.

Rule Two: A man should make an honest effort to get the names of his wife's friends right. This is not easy. The average wife who was graduated from school at any time during the past 30 years keeps in close touch with at least seven old classmates. These ladies, known as "the girls," are named, respectively: Mary, Marian, Melissa, Marjorie, Maribel, Madeleine and Miriam; and all of them are called Myrtle by the careless husband we are talking about.

Rule Three: A husband should not insult his wife publicly. Thus, if a man thinks the soufflés his wife makes are as tough as an outfielder's glove, he should tell her so when they are at home, not when they are out at a formal dinner where a perfect soufflé has just been served.

Rule Four: The wife who keeps saying, "Isn't that just like a man?" and the husband who keeps saying, "Oh, well, you know how women are," are likely to grow farther and farther apart through the years. These famous generalizations have the effect of reducing an individual to the anonymous status of a mere unit in a mass. The wife who, just in time, comes upon her husband about to fry an egg

in a dry skillet should not classify him with all other males but should give him the accolade of a special distinction. She might say, for example, "George, no other man in the world would try to do a thing like that." Similarly, a husband watching his wife laboring to start the car without turning on the ignition should not say to the gardener or a passerby, "Oh, well, you know, etc." Instead, he should remark to his wife, "I've seen a lot of women in my life, Nellie, but never one who could touch you."

Rule Five: A husband should try to remember where things are around the house so that he does not have to wait for his wife to get home from the hairdresser's before he can put his hands on what he wants. Among the things a husband is usually unable to locate are the iodine, the aspirin, the nail file, the French vermouth, his cuff links, black silk socks and evening shirts, the snapshots taken at Nantucket last summer, the garage key, the poker chips, his new raincoat and the screens for the upstairs windows. I don't really know the solution to this problem, but one should be found. Perhaps every wife should draw for her husband a detailed map of the house, showing clearly the location of everything he might need. Trouble is, I suppose, he would lay the map down somewhere and not be able to find it until his wife got home.

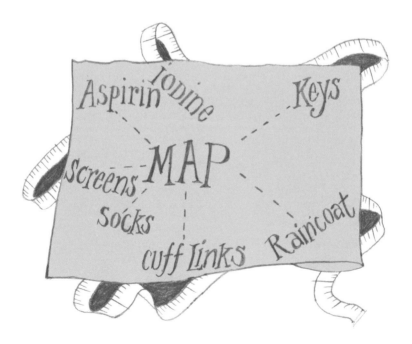

Rule Six: If a husband is not listening to what his wife is saying, he should not grunt, "Okay" or "Yeah, sure" or make little affirmative noises. A husband lost in thought or worry is likely not to take in the sense of such a statement as this: "We're going to the Gordons' for dinner tonight, John, so don't come home from the office first. Remember, we both have to be at the dentist's at five, and I'll pick you up there with the car." Now, an "Okay" or a "Yeah, sure" at this point can raise havoc if the husband hasn't really been listening. As usual, he goes all the way out to his home in Glenville—13 miles from the dentist's office and 17 miles from the Gordons' house—and he can't find his wife. His wife can't get him on the phone because all she gets is the busy buzz. John is calling everybody he can think of except, of course, the dentist and the Gordons. At last he hangs up, exhausted and enraged. Then the phone rings. It is his wife. And here let us leave them.

Rule Seven: A wife's dressing table should be inviolable. It is the one place in the house a husband should get away from and stay away from, and yet the average husband is drawn to it as by a magnet, especially when he is carrying something wet, oily, greasy or sticky, such as a universal joint, a hub cap or the blades of a lawn mower.
Now I realize, in glancing back over these rules, that some of my solutions to marital problems may seem a little untidy; that I have, indeed, left a number of loose ends here and there. For example, if the husbands are going to mislay their detailed maps of household objects, I have accomplished nothing except to add one item for the distraught gentleman to lose. I can only hope in conclusion, that this treatise itself will not start, in any household, a widening gap that can never be closed.

James Thurber

PROBLEMS OF BEING A PERFECT HUSBAND

I hate to admit it, but I'm the perfect husband. I'm not being conceited, nor am I necessarily bragging, because I know that being a perfect husband is a God-given talent, and you're either born with it or you're not. The perfect husband is one who is able to see his wife's faults, correct them if they need correcting, show her what she is doing wrong.

Marriage counselors will tell you that the happiest unions are those in which one of the mates is perfect and the other is not. Most marriages go on the rocks when both mates are perfect or both imperfect. I was lucky to find an imperfect wife, and as a result we've had a very happy marriage. It isn't easy to be the perfect husband. For one thing, you have to be *right* all the time, and it can be embarrassing when you constantly have to point out to your wife her mistakes. Occasionally, she gets exasperated and shouts, "If I could win an argument just once—that's all I ask. Let me win just once!"

I would love her to win an argument; but how can I when she's always wrong? I could fake it, I guess, and pretend she was right; but how can a wife respect a man who is wrong?

Let me cite some of the problems that a perfect husband faces.

As the perfect husband, I have had, on occasion, to point out to my wife the faults in her relatives. Sometimes she feels the criticism is unjust. But I explain to her that she is blinded by familial love, and since I am not related to any of her people, it is easier for me to see what's wrong with them.

If one is perfect in his home life, he should also be perfect in his social life. At parties, I am most flattering to the ladies. My wife has always felt that at a party I should pay more attention to her, and some of our fights have been over the attentions I have paid other women.

It's hard for her to understand that, since I am the perfect husband, she shouldn't be selfish about me. Some of the women I talk to may not have perfect husbands of their own and may need a friendly ear or a sympathetic smile. But all my wife gets out of it is that I'm flirting.

Some men think that to be a perfect husband they have to help around the house, cut the lawn, take out the garbage, clean the cellar, repair the roof. This is nonsense. Kings don't stand guard duty; presidents don't shovel snow; prime ministers don't wash their own cars. If you're the perfect husband, you must insist on dignity and delegate authority. Let people with imperfections do the dirty work.

If you're married to the perfect man, you probably have recognized in your own husband all the traits that I have pointed out here. If you're not, aren't you sorry that you're not married to me?

Art Buchwald

HAPPILY MARRIED

Every successful marriage works for different reasons. In the following excerpts from interviews, some famous happily marrieds speak for themselves.

Well, I really love Rosalynn more now than I did when I first married her. And I have loved no other woman except her. I had gone out with all kinds of girls, sometimes fairly steadily, but I just never cared about them. Rosalynn had been a friend of my sister's and was three years younger than I, which is a tremendous chasm in the high school years. She was just one of those insignificant little girls around the house. Then, when I was twenty-one, and home from the Navy on leave, I took her to the movies. Nothing extraordinary happened, but the next morning I told my mother, "That's the girl I want to marry." It's the best thing that ever happened to me.

We also share a religious faith, and the two or three times in our married life when we've had a serious crisis, I think that's what sustained our marriage and helped us overcome our difficulty. Our children, too, have been a factor binding Rosalynn and me together. After the boys, Amy came along late and it's been especially delightful for me, maybe because she's a little girl.

Jimmy Carter

Marriage is togetherness, in good and in bad. If you're together in good times, you take care of each other in bad times, too.

Sophia Loren

A big problem between any two people, especially in marriage, (is) communicating. T.S. Eliot said, 'We die to each other daily'—which is true. We're constantly changing, there's a constant readaption taking place. And *that* is what keeps a marriage alive and, when you catch up, it keeps you in love.

Princess Grace of Monaco

When I ask Carol (Burnett) to explain what needs her marriage fulfills, there is a long pause and then . . . "My need to have a date for Saturday nights!" she laughs. "Wouldn't it be awful to have to go through all that dating stuff again; wondering who would call and would he have a car and would he try to get fresh? Ugh! The thought is awful!" Then Carol becomes serious: "We allow one another to be—just to be," she says. "We ask nothing of one another that we first don't ask of ourselves. Those are gifts, you know. Gifts. There has never been a doubt in my mind that Joe and I could make it forever. I can't imagine a problem arising in our lives that would be insurmountable. You asked what marriage fulfills in me. How does anyone really answer such a question? It's an anchor, a comfort— companionship of the kind I wish for everyone.

"I know," says Carol, "that this will sound horribly 'itsy-poo,' but there is nothing lacking in my life, nothing further I could wish for. I have everything. And I'm not talking about money or fame, but about Joe and the children. Knowing someone cares for you, loves you—someone who you care for and love—what else is there?"

Alan Ekert

In a good marriage I think that adjustments between man and wife never cease; they simply grow smaller as the years go by.

June Haver MacMurray

DIFFERENCES ADD STRENGTH

A traveler in a foreign country who fears or fights the differences in its culture does not enjoy his trip nearly so much as the traveler who accepts, respects and even enjoys those differences. Much the same is true in marriage. If two people are exactly alike (which of course no two people are but which some couples seem determined to become), they limit their potential. Differences, when both husband and wife have learned how to deal with them, add not only interest to marriage but also strength.

Marcia Lasswell and Norman Lobsenz

WHY DOES ONE MARRY, ANYWAY?

In the following letter, Anne Morrow Lindbergh shares her thoughts on her upcoming marriage with a friend.

Corliss, it was so nice to see you again. I would have liked to have a long talk with you and would like to now. Apparently I am going to marry Charles Lindbergh. It must seem hysterically funny to you as it did to me, when I consider my opinions on marriage. "A safe marriage," "things in common," "liking the same things," "a quiet life," etc., etc. All those things which I am apparently going against. But they seem to have lost their meaning, or have other definitions. Isn't it funny—*why does* one marry, anyway? I didn't expect or want anything like this. I think probably that was the trouble. It must be fatal to decide on the kind of man you *don't* want to marry and the kind of life you *don't* want to lead. You determinedly turn your back on it, set out in the opposite direction—and come bang up against it, in true *Alice in the Looking Glass* fashion. And there he is—darn it all—the great Western strong-man-open-spaces type and a life of relentless action! But after all, what am I going to do about it? After all, there he is and I've got to go. I wish I could hurry up and get it over with soon. This horrible, fantastic, absurd publicity and thousands of people telling me how lucky and happy I am.

Corliss, if you write me and wish me conventional happiness, I will *never* forgive you. Don't wish me happiness—I don't expect to be happy, but it's gotten beyond that, somehow. Wish me courage and strength and a sense of humor—I will need them all.

Funny, my writing to you this way. But I could not write you a conventional "He-is-just-fine" letter. I feel as if I knew you so well. Corliss, you will not show this or quote it to anyone, will you? It would be awful if it got into the papers—as everything seems to. I don't mind if you tell Margaret, for I trust her and like her.

I can't leave this with an utterly frivolous picture of him. He is so much more than that. But talking about a person is almost always futile. Just reserve your opinions, Corliss, until you meet him. Newspaper accounts, casual acquaintance opinions, friendly articles about him are so utterly wrong.

He has vision and a sense of humor and extraordinarily nice eyes!

And that is enough to say now.

WE PLAYED IT BY EAR

Let me say at the beginning that much of the advice now freely given in print on the subject of marriage is just so much malarkey. One of the chief factors that contributed to a happy marriage in our household is that neither my bridegroom nor I had ever read any of those paralyzing tracts on marriage before we exchanged vows. If in 1929 there was a Spock on Spousery, we were happily unaware of it. We just got married and played it by ear.

Only the other day a female expert urged, in print, that a wife be "a hundred women" to her husband, possibly a Turk. A hundred women! Just being one woman exhausts me. And if my husband came home from the office some evening and found me prowling around in a leopard-skin leotard and a sequin blouse, with a rose in my teeth, he'd be terrified. The last thing in the world Add wants when he comes home is a New Woman. What he craves on the threshold is peace and the Same Old Familiar Face. He doesn't want to have to guess if this is Mata Hari night. Also, I do not hold with the admonition that a husband must woo his wife in perpetuity, or vice versa. Certainly I don't want to be treated like a caught streetcar. But, in turn, I can think of no prospect more dismal or more certain to blight tender domesticity than having a perpetual Romeo in the home. There is a time for poetry in marriage, but there also comes a time when the roast ought to be on the table. Marriage is for adults.

Two remarks made by my witty and beautiful Aunt Nell, when I was at an impressionable age, were worth all the professional marriage counseling I might have had, and taught me far more about human relationships in marriage. Aunt Nell was married happily for almost 50 years to one of the most delightful men I have ever known. But one day she confided, "There are days when I want to kill your uncle, but I am always glad the next morning that I stayed my hand."

On the second occasion, she burst into the house after a bridge party to say that her partner had complained all afternoon because she was misunderstood by her husband. Aunt Nell sighed happily and said, "I thank God daily that your uncle doesn't understand me. If he did, he'd leave home without even stopping to pack."

Inez Robb

TWO EQUALS ONE

Marriage is an individual matter, a matter of two separate people who make a singular couple. Victoria Lincoln said it a quarter of a century ago, best-selling author Dr. Wayne Dyer says it today.

My mother once told me about an elderly Boston spinster who said to her, "The trouble with marriage is that it breaks down the natural barrier between the sexes."
It does more than that. It breaks down the barriers between two human souls. And the greatest adventure and joy of life is that of learning, without illusions, to know another person and to love him as he really is.
There aren't any rules for that kind of happiness. For every marriage is as individual as the two individual lives that make it. And its own singular quality can only be learned in the actual living.

A relationship based on love is one in which each partner allows the other to be what he chooses, with no expectations and no demands. It is a simple association of two people who love each other so much that each would never expect the other to be something that he wouldn't choose for himself. It is a union based on independence, rather than dependence.

IT DOESN'T END, OF COURSE

It doesn't end.

In all growing
from all earths
to all skies,

in all touching
all things,

in all soothing
the aches of all years,

it doesn't end.

Simon Oritz

TO-NIGHT

The moon is a curving flower of gold,
    The sky is still and blue;
The moon was made for the sky to hold,
    And I for you.

The moon is a flower without a stem,
    The sky is luminous;
Eternity was made for them,
    To-night for us.

Sara Teasdale

TIME'S WAY

When all is said
& done
then we shall stand
as one

James Ryan Morris

SO NICE TO KNOW YOU

Sometimes I hardly think of you,
things get in the way.
The sights and sounds
of the average day
and the people I meet
all crowd between us,
and I seem to lose sight of your face.
But, now and then
in the stillness of a place,
I remember you,
and, as the sleeping bough quickens
when spring glances,
out of the still night,
thoughts of you begin
like distant singing voices.

Lily O'Sullivan

EVERY LOVE STORY IS SPECIAL

When the editors of the Farm Journal wanted to hear about happy marriages, over 400 "love letters" were received. The following excerpts are a testimony to the meaning of marriage in good times and in tight times.

"Any good love story has a hero, and that part is played by the man you married. He's the hard-hearted character who thinks Christmas is a lot of foolishness, then at the last minute goes on a spending spree. 'Kids need a little foolish stuff,' he will say, 'and Christmas comes but once a year.' There are so many instances like this one when you can stand apart, sort of, and think to yourself how exactly right this marriage is!"

It's the little thoughtful things a man does that mean so much to a woman. For instance, an unexpected gift—a husband's way of saying "I love you."

"Have you ever received a large hornet's nest for a birthday present?" asks one homemaker. "Love from a man

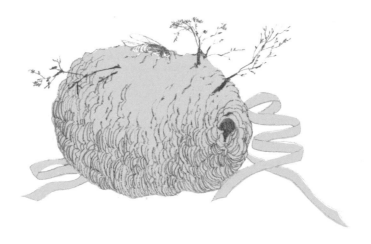

who sees beauty even in a hornet's nest is a very special kind of love." "When my husband worked nights," writes another, "there came a subscription to a book-every-month club so I wouldn't be so lonely evenings."

"How does my husband show his love? Not in the usual candy, flowers and compliments way. I know I'm loved when I fall asleep on the couch and wake to find his jacket covering me from drafts."

Sharing is a wonderful part of marriage, readers point out: "If anything interests him, he comes and tells me so I can enjoy it, too." . . . "When my husband's hand clasps mine in prayer, I know we have nothing to fear."

"True love is not a flame that dies out the first time a water pipe bursts or the pump won't pump. It's an ember kind of love which glows and grows when properly kindled. Glows with a touch of sentiment and grows stronger with each testing."

"No one knows that if my husband brings home only seven carnations for our anniversary, that's all the money he has. And what does it matter—when love is behind it all?"

"My husband accumulated an enormous amount of mileage meeting me more than halfway!" writes one wife.

"He stays amazingly cheerful when the rest of us blow up over losing billfolds or dropping our glasses in 12 feet of water while fishing. It's such morale-building that makes the difference between having a real husband or merely a man around the house!"

ALL YOU NEED IS LOVE . . .

Equality never will change the fact that it's love that makes the world go round.

Letitia Baldridge

If a couple share a sense of humor, they can usually manage to overcome any difference they may have over the problems that are bound to arise in normal life.

Dr. Joyce Brothers

True love is the ripe fruit of a lifetime.

Lamartine

Love is the star men look up to as they walk along, and marriage is the orbit they fall into.

Charles Kennedy

Marriage is an adventure in cooperation. The more we share the richer we will be; and the less we share the poorer we will be.

Harold B. Walker

A successful marriage requires falling in love many times with the same person.

Mignon McLaughlin

A good marriage is that in which each appoints the other guardian of his solitude. Once the realization is accepted that even between the closest human beings infinite distances continue to exist, a wonderful living side by side can grow up, if they succeed in loving the distance between them which makes it possible for each to see the other whole and against a wide sky.

Rainer Maria Rilke

SONG

What should a woman sing but love?
It is her cloak to keep her warm,
The scarlet hood about her head
That shelters her from storm.

It is the ribbon on her dress,
The book in which her fate is read,
The ring of gold upon her hand,
The dish from which her heart is fed.

Elizabeth Coatsworth

LOVE AT FIRST SIGHT

How do people meet—and marry? Every encounter is unique, and yet similar. John Denver tells of meeting his wife, the inspiration for his popular love song "Annie's Song."

"We did our concert and then the students did their show, and one skit had this girl who came up with signs like 'Act One' 'Act Two' 'Applause.' She was wearing jeans and a red shirt and had beautiful dark wavy hair, and she looked so alive. That caught me. I fell in love with her right then.

"But I couldn't figure out how to meet her. I'm shy with women unless it's business. I kept hanging around and pretty soon some students asked me to sing, and then she joined the group. Well, I sang every song to her.

"I told her who I was. Later I sent her a Christmas card with my name and address on it. She didn't answer. About a year later in October 1966, we were doing a concert in Minneapolis, and we had to drive through St. Peter to get there. I'd never forgotten about Annie and I was telling one of the other guys about her and he was impressed.

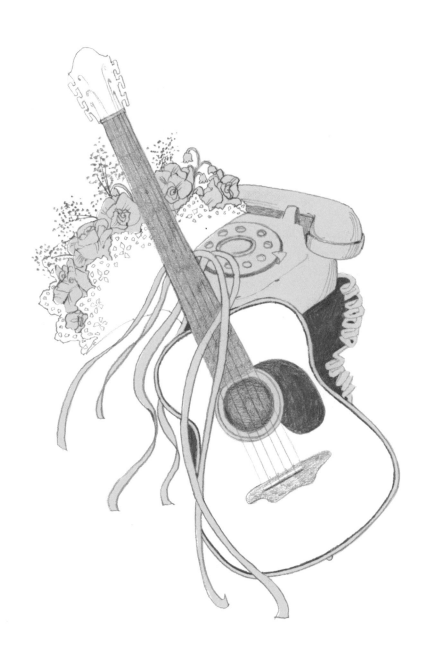

Man, imagine remembering one girl for a whole year!
"He got her phone number for me from some girl student.
I called and said, 'You won't remember me. I'm John
Denver. Do you want to come to my concert? When she
said 'yes,' I think I drove eighteen miles to her sorority
house in eighteen minutes.
"Two nights later I invited her to another concert fifty
miles away and she came, and I was hooked. I had it so
bad I flew to St. Peter between concerts and when bad
weather grounded all the planes, I took a train to see her
for a day.
"Just before Christmas of 1966, I was in Los Angeles and
the Trio was having trouble, and I was homesick and love-
sick. So I called her and invited myself over to her house
for Christmas. That's when I found out she was going to a
place called Aspen the following month with her college ski
club. I decided to tag along."
Once there, John went crazy about the beauty of Aspen.
He told himself that when he had money, this is where he
wanted to live and settle down. With Annie, of course.
Back on the bus to Minnesota, John proposed. She said,
"No." He told her that he wouldn't ask again unless he was
certain the answer was "Yes." John didn't phone for a
month and then a friend of hers called to tell John that
Annie was lonely. He raced to the phone and proposed
once more. Annie said "Yes."
The wedding, a church wedding, took place June 9, 1967 in
St. Peter, Minnesota. The bride wore a white lace gown
with a chiffony veil. John wore (would you believe?) a cut-
away tux, vest, Ascot tie, and flower in his lapel. He
resembled an All-American boy with a crewcut, and a grin
you can see in a million wedding photographs. He says he
hasn't worn a suit since.

David Dachs

APOLOGY FOR HUSBANDS

In answer to a friend's observation that they're
"more bother than they're worth"

Although your major premise, dear,
    Is rather sharp than subtle,
My honest argument, I fear,
    Can offer scant rebuttal.

I grant the Husband in the Home
    Disrupts its neat machinery.
His shaving brush, his sorry comb,
    Mar tidy bathroom scenery.

When dinner's prompt upon the plate,
He labors at the office late;
Yet stay him while the stew is peppered,
He rages like a famished leopard.
He rages like an angry lion
When urged to put a formal tie on,
But should festivities grow hearty,
He is the last to leave the party.
He lauds your neighbor's giddy bonnet
But laughs, immoderate, if you don it,
And loathes your childhood friend, and always
Bestrews his garments through the hallways.

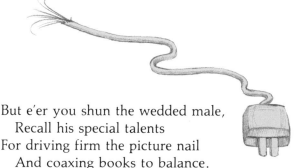

But e'er you shun the wedded male,
  Recall his special talents
For driving firm the picture nail
  And coaxing books to balance.

Regard with unalloyed delight
  That skill, which you were scorning,
For opening windows up at night
  And closing them at morning.

Though under protest, to be sure,
He weekly moves the furniture.
He layeth rugs, he fixeth sockets,
He payeth bills from both his pockets.
For invitations you decry
He furnisheth an alibi.
He jousts with taxi-men in tourney,
He guards your luggage when you journey,
And brings you news and quotes you facts
And figures out the income tax
And slaughters spiders when you daren't
And makes a very handy parent.

What gadget's useful as a spouse?
  Considering that a minute,
Confess that every proper house
  Should have a husband in it.

Phyllis McGinley

LIKE RAINING IN A RIVER

Like raining in a river; like the dove,
The mourning dove, when day already dies;
Like dawn at noon were there a sun to rise—
But oh, there is, and she is my own love—
Like dreams in dreams her bounty is, above
All asking, and all wanting, were I wise;
But I am not, and so it multiplies—
My happiness, that nothing will remove.

It is the child of such a sweet excess
In her that loves me, it can never end.
See how she tries, by giving, to be less,
Yet grows; and so my love does, that is friend
To trees and stars, those great ones who confess
All night how far love's limits do extend.

Mark Van Doren

LOVE, SHMOVE

"Compatibility" in marriage didn't always mean what it does today. And marital happiness and love weren't as openly discussed—but they were there. Humorist Sam Levenson tells how it really was with his Mama and Papa.

It was hard to tell whether the papas and mamas of that era were happily married. The subject was not open for discussion, certainly not with their children.

"Are you happy, Ma?"

"I got nothing else to think about?"

Nobody had ever told Mama that marriage was supposed to make her happy; certainly Papa hadn't. Nobody had promised *him* happy either. Mature people prayed for good health, good fortune, and an honorable old age. A husband was supposed to make a living, and a wife was supposed to make a life of it. Only children talked of happiness; they still believed in fairy tales. Human beings, the

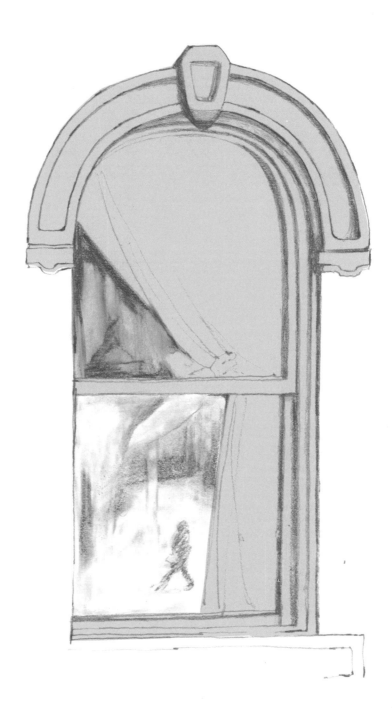

old folks said, don't live happily forever after, most of the time not even during, so it was wise in marriage and in everything else to expect the worst. Then if it turned out to be only worse, it still wasn't too bad. Marriage was one of those things you were supposed to save for your old age, happy or not.

"Love, shmove!" Papa used to say. "I love blintzes; did I marry one?" The word "love" embarrassed them. It was an unmentionable, like "brassiere," "hernia," and "miscarriage." Not that they didn't believe in love. They felt it, but avoided the precise definition that young people demand. Defining it might lead to misunderstanding rather than understanding. Defining it might even diminish it. To Mama love was not passion, or infatuation, or compatibility. She had given birth to ten kids without any of those. "Love," said Mama after many years of marriage, "is what you have been through with someone."

Love was made up of satisfaction ("Ten kids, thank God, is plenty"), sharing ("If he can take it, I can take it"), optimism ("Worse it couldn't get!"), and friendship, not in the style of Romeo and Juliet or Tristan and Isolde, but more like Damon and Pythias.

I knew my parents valued each other, because Papa told me always to listen to Mama and Mama told me always to listen to Papa; because whenever a decision was to be made regarding me, Mama said, "We'll ask Papa," and Papa said, "We'll ask Mama"; because Mama always watched at the window when Papa left for work and whispered to herself about his being "a good man, a learned man, to work so hard in a shop, it's a pity"; because at lunchtime she had me deliver a pot of hot soup two miles in the snow to Papa's shop so "he should know"; because Papa wouldn't spend a penny on himself unless Mama spent on herself. Share and share alike. So the day Mama had all her teeth pulled, Papa bought a suit.

LOVE IN A NUTSHELL

At a recent football game, I overheard one wife say to another, "I know your husband is crazy about football. Are you a football nut, too?" The other wife smiled and replied, "I love my husband."

Mrs. Albert Einstein was asked, "Do you understand your husband's theory of relativity?" She smiled, "Oh, my, no, I just know how he likes his tea." That's love in a nutshell.

Marabel Morgan

WHAT IS A GOOD MARRIAGE

A good marriage offers a man and woman the best of everything: a steadfast ally against the world, a gracious and charming companion, sexual satisfaction, and a partner in the dazzling miracle of creating new human beings. Obviously, not every marriage can achieve all these things. But nearly every marriage provides the *chance* for a man and woman to grow closer and more loving with each passing year, and to find in one another the fulfillment of every human need.

David Reuben, M.D.

WHO CAN LOVE?

Are those who fall in love,
    Only youths of tender years,
Who've never experienced heartbreak,
    Or neglect, abuse and tears?

To love especially for the young?
    Their hearts the only ones that need
Dreams, fantasies and future hopes
    Upon which to feed?

No, Love, I can tell you this,
    This is true, you will find,
That youth relates not to age,
    But is a state of mind.

Everyone has the right to love,
    Despite their age in years,
To love and care for someone,
    Precludes a lonely vale of tears.

Your love and mine together
    Will grow deeper with the years,
Our trust in one another,
    Will banish any fears.

Charles C. Gage

LOVE'S GARDEN

Flowers that bloom in the Springtime.
  Flowers that bloom in the fall.
But the flowers of love in one's heart,
  Are the sweetest flowers of all.

Flowers of love last forever.
  They do not live just a day.
Nor wilt as the sun disappears,
  Nor wither and fade away.

No, flowers of love are deep-rooted,
  In the love garden of one's heart.
There entwined with the one who loves.
  Where nothing can sever apart.

Iola L. Slater

GOODNIGHT

This day is almost done. When the night and morning meet it will be only an unalterable memory. So let no unkind word; no careless, doubting thought; no guilty secret; no neglected duty; no wisp of jealous fog becloud its passing. For we belong to each other—to have and to hold—and we are determined not to lose the keen sense of mutual appreciation which God has given us. To have is passive, and was consummated on our wedding day, but to hold is active and can never be quite finished so long as we both shall live.

Now, as we put our arms around each other, in sincere and affectionate token of our deep and abiding love, we would lay aside all disturbing thoughts, all misunderstandings, all unworthiness. If things have gone awry let neither of us lift an accusing finger nor become entangled in the rationalizations of self-defense. Who is to blame is not important; only how shall we set the situation right. And so, serving and being served, loving and being loved, blessing and being blessed, we shall make a happy, peaceful home, where hearts shall never drop their leaves, but where we and our children shall learn to face life joyfully, fearlessly, triumphantly, so near as God shall give us grace. Goodnight, beloved.

F. Alexander Magoun

AMONG OTHER THOUGHTS ON OUR WEDDING ANNIVERSARY

Over the years,
When the sink overflowed
Or the car ran out of gas
Or the lady who comes every Tuesday to clean didn't come
Or I felt pudgy
Or misunderstood
Or inferior to Marilyn Kaufman who is not only a pediatric
    surgeon but also a very fine person as well as beautiful
Or I fell in the creek and got soaked on our first family
    camping trip
Or mosquitoes ate me alive on our first family camping trip
Or I bruised my entire left side on our first family camping
    trip
Or I walked through a patch of what later turned out to be
    plenty of poison ivy on what later turned out to be our
    last family camping trip

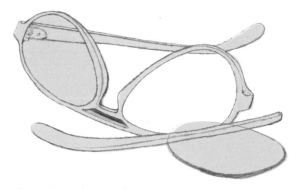

Or my sweater shrank in the wash
Or I stepped on my glasses
Or the keys that I swear on my children's head I put on the
    top of the dresser weren't there
Or I felt depressed
Or unfulfilled
Or inferior to Ellen Jane Garver who not only teaches con-
    stitutional law but is also a wit plus sexually insatiable
Or the rinse that was going to give my hair some subtle
    copper highlights turned it purple
Or my mother-in-law got insulted at something I said
Or my stomach got upset at something I ate
Or I backed into a truck that I swear when I looked in my
    rear-view mirror wasn't parked there
Or I suffered from some other blow of fate,
It's always been so nice to have my husband by my side so
    I could
Blame him.

Judith Viorst

SEPTEMBER

Yesterday the pears were hard,
    Too green for raiding;
Today they're honey in the mouth.
    Summer is fading.

Yesterday green leaves
    Dappled the lawn,
Now green leaves are russet,
    Summer is gone.

Yesterday was blade-bright
    Beneath a metal sun;
That bronze is hazed today,
    Autumn is come.

Bronze haze and pear juice,
    Cold till after ten;
Autumn is a new year,
    Let's begin again.

Jessamyn West

WE HAVE LIVED AND LOVED TOGETHER

We have lived and loved together
   Through many changing years;
We have shared each other's gladness
   And wept each other's tears;
I have known ne'er a sorrow
   That was long unsoothed by thee;
For thy smiles can make a summer
   Where darkness else would be.

Like the leaves that fall around us
   In autumn's fading hours,
Are the traitor's smiles, that darken
   When the cloud of sorrow lowers;
And though many such we've known love,
   Too prone, alas, to range,
We both can speak of one love
   Which time can never change.

We have lived and loved together
   Through many changing years;
We have shared each other's gladness
   And wept each other's tears.
And let us hope the future,
   As the past has been will be;
I will share with thee my sorrows,
   And thou thy joys with me.

Charles Jefferys

ACKNOWLEDGMENTS

The editor and the publisher have made every effort to trace the owner-ship of all copyrighted material and to secure permission from copyright holders of such material. In the event of any question arising as to the use of any material the publisher and editor, while expressing regret for inadvertent error, will be pleased to make the necessary corrections in future printings. Thanks are due to the following authors, publishers, publications and agents for permission to use the material indicated.

RICHARD ARMOUR, for "Going Concern" from *Nights with Armour* by Richard Armour, published by McGraw-Hill, 1958.

ART BUCHWALD, for excerpt from "The Problems of Being a Perfect Husband," published in the July 1963 issue of *McCalls*.

CITADEL PRESS, INC., for excerpt from *The Wit and Wisdom of Jimmy Carter* edited by Bill Adler.

THE CONDÉ NAST PUBLICATIONS, INC., for excerpt from "What Makes a Happy Marriage" by Victoria Lincoln, published in the August 1, 1954 issue of *Vogue*. Copyright© 1954 by The Condé Nast Publications, Inc.

THOMAS Y. CROWELL CO., INC., for excerpt from *Your Erroneous Zones* by Wayne Dyer. Copyright© 1976 by Wayne Dyer.

T. S. DENISON & COMPANY, INC., for "We Have Lived and Loved Together" by Charles Jefferys from *Wedding Anniversary Celebrations* by Beatrice Plumb and Mabel Fuller.

DOUBLEDAY & COMPANY, INC., for excerpt ("Differences Add Strength") from *No-Fault Marriage* by Marcia Lasswell and Norman M. Lobsenz. Copyright© 1976 by Marcia Lasswell and Norman M. Lobsenz.

DOWNE PUBLISHING, INC., for excerpt from article on Carol Burnett by Alan Ebert, published in the December 1976 issue of *Ladies' Home Journal*. Copyright© 1976 by Downe Publishing, Inc. Reprinted with permission of *Ladies' Home Journal*.

FARM JOURNAL, for excerpts from article on Love Letters published in the February 1959 issue. Copyright© 1959 by *Farm Journal*.

HARCOURT BRACE JOVANOVICH, INC., for excerpt ("Why Does One Marry, Anyway?") from *Bring Me A Unicorn* by Anne Morrow Lindbergh. Copyright© 1971, 1972 by Anne Morrow Lindbergh; for "September" from *The Secret Look* by Jessamyn West. Copyright© 1952 by Jessamyn West; for excerpt from *John Denver* by David Dachs. Copyright© 1976 by David Dachs. Reprinted by permission of Jove Publications, Inc., (a subsidiary of Harcourt Brace Jovanovich, Inc.).

HARPER & ROW, PUBLISHERS, INC., for "Goodnight" from *Love and Marriage* by F. Alexander Magoun. Copyright© 1936 by F. Alex-

Selected by Barbara Shook Hazen
Designed by Al Petersen
Illustrations by Blanche Sims